C I R F A C T S

Sternberg Press

CONTENTS

CIRCULAR FACTS

Mai Abu ElDahab, Binna Choi,
& Emily Pethick

THE SHOWROOM, LONDON × × CASCO, UTRECHT × OBJECTIF EXHIBITIONS, ANTWERP

THE PERIOD IN WHICH WE STARTED developing the idea for the joint project Circular Facts* was a changing moment for each of our thinking about how small-scale organizations function. In this book we have brought together a group of curators, directors, and collaborators, each of whose working methods we feel connected to, as a way to introduce some of the issues that we are collectively concerned with to a broader public and to discuss the role of small organizations in the cultural field and how they envision the future.

There are four central issues we are interested in tackling. Firstly, as we face impending (if not already present) funding problems as the current global financial crises drip down into public sector cuts, the conditions that we're working under are changing dramatically. In this climate we feel it pertinent to look at the factors that in our view define our relevance as publicly-funded organizations. Secondly, we need to qualify our relationship to the public. Thirdly, having been initiated and developed under very different political conditions, small organizations formerly acted as direct conduits between critical cultural thinking and policymakers in much less institutionalized landscapes. Today we are being steered towards the idea that artistic and curatorial practice must see its future within the neoliberal business model. Lastly, we wanted to speculate on our future, or perhaps invent it ourselves, by questioning the premises upon which we articulate our positions,

* The title Circular Facts is borrowed from a work by participating artist Ruth Buchanan.

and how we work and participate in both the art world and public life.

We summarized our thoughts into the following questions, which we used to brief the book's contributors:

× From your own experience, what are the roles, qualities, and impacts of small-scale art organizations in relation to the local art scene, international art world, and the cultural field at large? How do these relationships define/affect the organization's working methods?

× How would you describe the existing and/or desired relationship between organizations and artists?

× Within the current political and financial climate, can you put forward a vision of what these small-scale institutions might transform into or what new functions they might take on?

Although many of the issues that are pertinent to the Circular Facts collaborators seem specific to working in a European context, we have invited a broad spectrum of writers from further afield in the hope that the articulation of diverse publics, contexts, working methods, and structures could form a collective view of our affinities and how we define what we do. The publication represents a variety of different organizational positions, including three perspectives from newly formed organizations – Anthony Huberman writing about The Artist's Institute, New York; Beatriz Cavia, Miren Jaio, Isabel de Naverán, and Leire Vergara writing about Bulegoa zenbaki barik, Bilbao; and Krist Gruijthuijsen and Maxine Kopsa writing about Kunstverein, Amsterdam – alongside Heejin Kim's essay on the artist-run space Art Space Pool, Seoul; Anna Colin and Mélanie Bouteloup on Bétonsalon, Paris; and a conversation with Kim Einarsson on Konsthall C, Stockholm.

This publication forms the second part of our attempt to address the role of small-scale organizations in the contemporary art world. In May 2011, we invited a group of curators to Antwerp to participate in what we called the Circular Facts: Public Meeting. This two-and-a-half day event at Objectif Exhibitions was spent discussing these very same issues, and inevitably it felt like the dense and fruitful beginning of a conversation rather than its conclusion. We have included selected extracts from the event that offer further perspectives on models of small organizations, with contributions by Nataša Petrešin-Bachelez on Les Laboratoires D'Aubervilliers, Paris; Francis McKee on CCA, Glasgow; and Will Bradley on Kunsthall Oslo. The diversity of positions represented in these excerpts and those in the commissioned texts very clearly demonstrate the versatility of small-scale organizations and the different kinds of challenges they are facing in relation to local contexts.

It is important also to note that this book is part of a larger project in which our three organizations – Casco – Office for Art, Theory and Design in Utrecht, Objectif Exhibitions in Antwerp, and The Showroom in London, along with our collaborators Kunsthalle Sankt Gallen and Electric Palm Tree – have been involved over the past three years. Circular Facts is a collaborative think tank and support structure that works as a hub for the production and dissemination of a series of artistic projects. Our emphasis has been on finding non-bureaucratic ways of working together and pooling resources to realize a pragmatic and sustainable model for coproduction based on our common interest in creating a climate conducive to artistic creativity and criticality. Our organizations have a common focus on supporting artistic practices that critically engage with ways of thinking around our contemporary conditions. Through our collaboration we've tried to facilitate and better understand these kinds of practices. Circular Facts has developed projects with Agency, Can Altay, Ei Arakawa, Petra Bauer, Ruth Buchanan, Norma Jeane, and Hassan Khan, and workshops that include Dexter Sinister's The Serving Library, Signal:Noise, and Electric Palm Tree.

We hope that both our project and this publication offer not only food for thought about the future of publicly-funded art spaces, but can also highlight the crucial role we believe they play in sowing the seeds for an effective and fruitful form of support for artists, art, and our audiences.

×
THE ARTIST'S INSTITUTE,
NEW YORK

TAKE CARE

Anthony Huberman

HOW TO WORK BETTER (1991) is a well-known work by Swiss artists Peter Fischli and David Weiss. It consists of a ten-point manifesto that the artists found, enlarged, and had painted on the side of a building in Zurich. Their instructions are meant as a self-motivating reminder and description of their own process as artists, but are also directed to the rest of the world as a propositional code of conduct or ethic of behavior – in fact, a copy of *How to Work Better* is pinned to the wall of countless artist studios around the world, as well as above the desks of many curators, including this one.

HOW TO WORK BETTER.

1 DO ONE THING AT A TIME
2 KNOW THE PROBLEM
3 LEARN TO LISTEN
4 LEARN TO ASK QUESTIONS
5 DISTINGUISH SENSE FROM NONSENSE
6 ACCEPT CHANGE AS INEVITABLE
7 ADMIT MISTAKES
8 SAY IT SIMPLE
9 BE CALM
10 SMILE

The question of how to work or how to behave is one that lies at the root of all of our decisions. To rehearse a common truism: it's not just what you do, it's how you do it – it's not just what artists or curators do, but how they behave when they do it. Beyond the different styles, techniques, or themes that characterize their work are the different codes of conduct that guide the way they act or behave. The same could be said of museums or art institutions: running alongside the question of what they are showing is the question of how they are behaving.

In recent years, small organizations around the world have been formulating different answers to that question. They are taking risks not just with what art to show but also with how to work and how to behave as an institution. In other words, in addition to having an adventurous and forward-thinking curatorial program, they are experimenting with new institutional and curatorial methodologies that articulate a new ethic of behavior and a new code of conduct. As a result, they are outlining a context for what it means to propose an alternative today. My own effort towards this, with The Artist's Institute in New York, is but one proposition among many others.

With mainstream museums and commercial galleries often showing uncommercial work by uncommercial artists, the role historically played by alternative spaces has been made somewhat redundant. Now is a time when MoMA shows performance art, the Whitney shows site-specific art, the Guggenheim shows institutional critique, and the New Museum shows artists who are "Younger Than Jesus" (2009). Commercial galleries such as Reena Spaulings or Alex Zachary allow the most prominent collectors to buy work by the most uncompromising artists. And those smaller organizations that manage to stay non-profit and independent soon find themselves invited by the Tate Modern for "No Soul for Sale" (2010) or by the ICA for "Nought to Sixty" (2008).

While these mainstream or commercial structures might take risks with what they show, few take risks with how they work. In most cases, they produce exhibitions, one after the other, and strategically compete for larger audiences and for more widespread recognition. The challenge for a contemporary alternative space or curatorial approach is to behave differently.

For example, the logic and structure of exhibitions could itself be called into question. Much of the difficulty with making an exhibition lies in the fact that to extract something from circulation – an object, image, practice, or idea – and interrupt it, examine it, and exhibit it, is to do it a great injustice. The philosopher Bruno Latour, among others, discusses the life of *things*, referring, in the largest sense, to all that which is usually not considered to be cognizant human subjects: objects, pictures, rocks, animals, natural systems, etc.[1] These things, he argues – objects, images, and ideas included – have their own agency and won't simply sit still under someone else's microscope, on someone else's terms. In fact, what makes them compelling is precisely what animates them, what they want, and how they behave when they are set loose into the world. In other words, objects, images, and ideas have lives to live, and instead of conceiving of an exhibition as a way to reign them in and use them to carefully prove a point, an exhibition could be something much riskier: a way to discover, along with the audience, how that point will behave and where it will wander as it lives its life. In this

1. See Bruno Latour, "From Realpolitik to Dingpolitik or How to Make Things Public," in *Making Things Public: Atmospheres of Democracy*, eds. Bruno Latour and Peter Weibel (Cambridge, MA: MIT Press, 2005), 14–41.

sense, the opening of an exhibition could mark the beginning of a curatorial idea, not its end.

Traditionally, it's the other way around: curators open their shows and play the role of explicators, working to enlighten visitors who don't know what they know. They are expert performers of the *I Know* and avoid displaying any sign of the *I Don't Know*. Instead, an alternative curatorial behavior could be to embrace a more vulnerable relationship to knowledge. An institution could stop behaving like an explanation machine, where those who know are teaching those who don't know, and invest in what philosopher Jacques Rancière calls the "equality of intelligences,"[2] where those who know something engage with those who know something *else*. It's not about preparing explanations in advance, but about following the life of an idea, in public, with others.

Clearly, the goal is not to reject the expertise of the *I Know* in favor of the anti-intellectualism of the *I Don't Know*, but to step outside of that binary entirely. Following the art critic Jan Verwoert,[3] it means performing both the *I Know* and the *I Don't Know* in the key of the *I Care*. Verwoert suggests the *I Care* as an act of giving what you don't have to people who don't want it, or, in other words, as an act that is more *affective* than it is *effective*. If an institution goes from knowing to caring, it could point to the affective relationship that ties people to ideas and become a place for attachment rather

---

2. See Jacques Rancière, *The Ignorant Schoolmaster: Five Lessons in Intellectual Emancipation* (Stanford, CA: Stanford University Press, 1991).
3. Jan Verwoert, "Exhaustion and Exuberance," *Dot Dot Dot* 15 (2007): 89–112.

than consumption. After all, the ideas that make us curious are not the ones we fully understand, but the ones we care about – *I Love It* is always more compelling than *I Get It*.

In unpacking the *I Care*, Verwoert also points to the importance of the figure of the muse: he or she who inspires and influences you – or, etymologically speaking, who amuses you. Funnily enough, one tends to think of the curator as being the artist's host, inviting him or her into an institution, but it's actually the other way around: we are the guests of the artists we choose to work with. In that context, like for any other houseguest, we should find a way to say *Thank You*. An exhibition could be an homage instead of a lesson – a way to thank artists, not dissect them.

Curatorial responsibility involves the invention of ways to appropriately pay tribute to the lives of artworks and artists – not the invention of curatorial methods for their own sake. By always putting the artist first, a good exhibition behaves like a guest who takes care to do whatever is true to the spirit of the work.

To pay homage to someone falls somewhere between admiring them and studying them. A tribute is neither an analysis nor just a party. Giving a toast is about making people care, not about making them understand. The act of appreciation, by nature, is not didactic – it's what you like, not what you know – but it is social: it involves not just what you like, but caring about it so much that you want to share it with others. It's more than naming a favorite book, it's recommending it. The affective curatorial approach of the *I Care* can inhabit that space between homage and explanation, between tribute and analysis, between recommendation and nomination. Once again, this is a place where the *I Know* coexists equally with the *I Don't Know* in the form of the *I Care.* While the uptown museums conduct their art historical power games and the downtown galleries conceive their elusive tactics and smart chess moves, those eager for another model could perform the vulnerable, dangerous, and radical act of wearing their heart on their sleeve.

While behaving in the key of the *I Care* can be an act of celebration, it can also be one of critique: the art of the toast is closely aligned with the art of the roast. An alternative and affective curatorial behavior involves the biting quip and critical edge of *parrhesia* – to use a term resurrected by Michel Foucault[4] – or fearless speech. To practice parrhesia is to have the courage to speak frankly from a position of exposed vulnerability. Unlike the careful and calculated strategies of a much safer practice of *rhetoric* – the debate of differences between equals – parrhesia involves a willingness to stand for irreverent or critical values from the perspective of a less powerful member of the community, and is certainly relevant to those smaller and more vulnerable institutions.

To care also means to take care and to pay attention, and in order to properly do that, as argued by philosopher Bernard Stiegler, we need to slow down and take our time.[5] While museums

---

4. See Michel Foucault, *Fearless Speech* (Los Angeles: Semiotexte(e), 2001).
5. See Bernard Stiegler, *Taking Care of Youth and the Generations* (Stanford, CA: Stanford University Press, 2010).

build more buildings, produce more exhibitions, raise more money, place more ads, and hope to draw more crowds, another model could be to do less and spend more time with what we do. Rather than feeding the conveyor belt of the *next, next, next*, we could stop channel surfing and demand a more focused and sustained attention span. One way organizations do this is by simply repeating themselves: for example, year after year, the commercial gallery Miguel Abreu in New York repeatedly hosts a screening of films by Jean-Marie Straub and Danièle Huillet, insisting on their sustained relevance to the gallery's identity and program as a whole. Another way many organizations take their time is by emphasizing research over exhibitions: if exhibitions traditionally last six to ten weeks, research-based initiatives allow for the pursuit of speculative questions over longer periods of time, leading to more in-depth and textured thinking. BAK, basis voor actuele kunst in Utrecht, for example, commits several years to thinking through a single theme through exhibitions, publications, conferences, or private roundtables, all placed on equal footing. Mamco in Geneva, although far from being a smaller alternative space, conceives of an exhibition as a single program that evolves over several years, made manifest in a series of episodes. Another mainstream yet relevant institution, the Dia Art Foundation in New York, not only presents single exhibitions that last a minimum of eight months, but is also committed to maintaining (and caring for) expensive long-term projects such as Walter De Maria's *The Lightning Field* (1977) or *Earth Room* (1977). While many galleries and art centers seem seduced by Hans Ulrich Obrist's *dontstopdontstopdontstop* (Sternberg Press, 2006), others aren't, and prefer to *stop*.

The media, of course, always favors the fast and the furious. Therefore, stepping off the conveyor belt also means falling out of the news cycle, and behaving this way will inevitably draw smaller audiences. This smaller scale does come with several advantages: not only is it much cheaper to maintain a smaller physical space, but this intimacy will also favor a face-to-face encounter and demand a more active and immediate engagement. Organizations such as Salon Populaire or Silberkuppe in Berlin, Kunstverein in Amsterdam, Pro Choice in Vienna, Front Desk Apparatus in New York, castillo/corrales in Paris, or New Jerseyy in Basel are no larger than 100 square meters, and are designed with that very characteristic in mind.

Since they invest in face time rather than in ad time, these small institutions build their audience as the result of a self-selecting process. In other words, the people who pay attention are not the ones who are encouraged to do so, but the ones who choose to do so. Since anyone is invited to attend any of the exhibitions or events, this is not a case of speakeasy or strategic exclusivity, but it effectively creates a space for self-selected and engaged community of people who care. The goal is not to engage in a competition to attract more audiences, but to establish a smaller gift economy for anyone who is curious enough and makes the effort to come by for a visit, whether a friend or a stranger.

More than anything, the challenge for a contemporary alternative space today is to behave the way Martin Luther King Jr. called upon *all* people to behave: to be maladjusted. By evoking a term usually associated with a psychological defect or illness, Dr. King famously declared that he was proud to be maladjusted, and that he would never adjust himself to a society that discriminates against racial minorities. In the art context, these smaller institutions are proud to be maladjusted: they do not adjust themselves to an art community obsessed with knowledge, power, and scale. Instead, they step onto the smaller and more vulnerable roads and allow learning to replace teaching, camaraderie to replace competition, the homage to replace the explanation, and the dance move to replace the chess move.

As a tribute to Fischli & Weiss, let me conclude and summarize by proposing an updated set of instructions for a contemporary ethic of curatorial behavior. It could certainly hang over the desk at The Artist's Institute.

HOW TO BEHAVE BETTER.

1 REMEMBER THAT YOU DON'T KNOW
2 LEARN TO CARE
3 SAY THANK YOU
4 WEAR YOUR HEART ON YOUR SLEEVE
5 INSIST ON TALKING FACE TO FACE
6 FOLLOW THE LIFE OF AN IDEA
7 SPEAK FRANKLY
8 TAKE YOUR TIME
9 BE MALADJUSTED
10 TOAST

RESILIENCE

Heejin Kim

THE FIRST QUESTION that I was asked to address in this publication concerned the role and impact of small-scale art organizations in relation to their local art scenes, the international art world, and the cultural field at large. As some art practitioners may know, the issue of translation is crucial in trans-contextual collaborations across regional borders, as is the case of Circular Facts. Translation is no longer conceived as a matter of commanding technical or scholarly language, but as a commitment to reconfigure general assumptions. In this framework, I would like to problematize the process of trans-positioning specific notions across different regional contexts and cultural orders, such as that of smallness in the context of art organizations. I will do so by discussing the conditions that surround the collective distrust in small art organizations in Seoul.

For the past two years, being a small actor in the cultural scene of this region has become synonymous with specific economic and political conditions: isolation from the general public and constraint from the national government. An exception lies in private galleries that intentionally take a small-scale approach to hide political connections and to evade heavy taxation, for example, by using the sale of artworks as a means of money laundering. There are also corporate cultural agencies who choose small-scale frames of action until they are proven profitable and their business plans are approved by their mother companies. Generally, however, the irresistible power of visibility in the visual art industry makes the popularity factor appear to be a more convincing model. Consequently, small organizations are deemed as lacking credibility and unreliable.

Behind the current obsessive desire for spectacularly bigger cultural bodies in Seoul lies the prosperity-driven policies of the current neoliberal populist regime. In 2009, the neoconservative government flagged its slogan of "prosperity" as a way to partly cover up the damages that they had created by their own choice of neoliberal economic policies. This was primarily in order to pay back its own group of supporters, the traditional conservative capitalists, who had been purposefully oblivious to the criminal record of the presidential candidate. As a result, the national policy was set for visible tangible prosperity within the five years of the official presidential period. To attain this goal, the state instantly launched a myriad of gigantic national construction plans. At the same time, in order to maintain the funding supply for this national enterprise, it enforced huge cuts in the social welfare budget and instigated the privatization of public properties. Taxation has been severed, the economic polarization intensified, the middle class diminished, and public funds have been directed towards politically-neutralized private initiatives.

At the same time, the state has propelled individual competition by means of various social campaigns that glorify survivors of seemingly infinite challenges, all promoted via national media. In the Seoul art scene there have been numerous award-offering initiatives that drive young emerging artists towards speedy career development, producing survival strategies that are more aligned with hit-and-run gambling than with long-term self-discipline. Recent events create a gloomy portrait of the region: a scriptwriter in her twenties was found dead from depression and malnutrition in Seoul; four super-elite students of KAIST (Korea Advanced Institute of Science & Technology) committed suicide in the space of one month due to the pressure caused by escalating tuition fees associated with academic performance; and, finally, the national bureau of statistics has artificially inflated the percentage of the country's middle class in order to sustain Korea's position as one of the most economically stable G20 countries. Materialism, populism, and conformity structure the Korean social value system.

What I am concerned about in this nationwide "Vanity Fair" is the suspicious vengeance of the conformed competitors upon the nonconformists. The blind collective logic goes as follows: because you don't make as much effort as us, you are either "social losers," "useless lumpen," "social misfits," or perhaps "the reds"; you deserve isolation and to be despised by the "general public." Hard to believe, but this is quite a common assumption in this politically divided state where fear is frequently mixed with ideological terror. Things that are incomplete, shabby, informal, and small are not only distrusted, but also isolated and hated. And, unsurprisingly in view of the current climate, artist groups are regarded among the major "social losers."

In the current psycho-political climate the fact that a public organization is small implies that it is fighting against multiple repulsions, be that from politicians, businessmen, or ordinary citizens – all whom characterize it as some kind of "dangerous public enemy."

At this point, I dare apply the term "ethical" to the insistence of being small. The act of staying small for public or semi-public organizations is ethical in that it is a public reminder that such attempts to maintain financial transparency and a sharpened critical awareness of the local political game (political spectacle, connection with econo-politicians, corruption, privileges, etc.), as well as to suggest that possible alternative value systems ought to exist.

Art Space Pool, where I work as director, has from the time of its establishment in 1999 always been "small," and it has not become dramatically bigger in the two remaining years of this presidential period. Pool, meaning "grass" in English, has assumed a core position in the local art scene, both as an intellectual and practical locus of grassroots cultural producers who share critical reflections on its surrounding reality. Its agenda, methodology, and approach are diverse, but the broadly grouped "Pool artists" include Yong-ik Kim, Chan-kyong Park, FlyingCity, Bae Young Whan, Koh Seung Wook, and Rho Jae Oon, to name a few. Any historical genealogy of critical art practice in modern and contemporary Korea would necessarily have to include them.

These artists cofounded and have co-run the organization over the past decade: in this sense, Pool's mission has been dedicated to supporting them with the production of new work, education, discourses, and networking. Currently, it also still profiles prominent local emerging artists and acts as an incubator for them through its educational and discursive programs, connecting artists to like-minded cultural practitioners. Rather than representing them commercially, Pool has advocated the autonomy of art in relation to the politicized market and institutionalized art productions. This has allowed it to disrupt the monocentric standards of high art and authoritative art systems governed by local political power. Although the agenda surrounding Pool has evolved in response to the local reality on a case-by-case basis, the rough strands of what has been addressed within the program include conceptual realism, post-colonialism, feminism, institutional critique, locality, social minorities, regional communities, and, most recently, knowledge production and creative capital.

When I began working at Pool in winter 2009 – almost one year after the presidential inauguration of 2008 – the organization was on the brink of closure due to the artists' frustration with imminent political censorship by the new government, and the reduction of public grants, upon which half of the art center's budget had depended.* Most critically, the great heritage of criticality within the local art scene was exhausted by deep frustration and a pervading sense of failure. This condition wasn't exclusive to Pool, but that of creative workers in general, who were burnt out, isolated, depressed, and trapped in a survival game ruled by extreme functionalism, pragmatism, material success, and spectacular visibility.

I found that the best way to overcome this situation was to look at what was already there. Pool is a great resource and is surrounded by a community with shared interests, experiences, and ideas. My immediate task was to restore to these cultural producers a sense of self-confidence and social pride. For this to happen, Pool strengthened its function as a community space, membership was enforced, and its members were made responsible for the fostering of mutual energy. Those who cannot afford a financial donation can contribute in kind by donating their artworks for sales, giving lectures, writing critical essays, being mentors for junior artists' collectives, or by helping out with installations, openings, or catering.

---

* For a detailed description of the political intervention in the cultural scene in 2009, please refer to my other essays, "Beyond Recurring Traumas and a New Scar: Notes on the Impoverished Public Art Infrastructure in Korea," *Diaaalogue*, December 2009, www.aaa.org.hk; and "The Reason Why We Support Geonggi Creative Center and Gyeonggi Museum of Modern Art," in *2009 RES ARTIS Conference: The 21st Century Art Residency and New Institutional Collaborations* (Ansan: Geonggi Creative Center, Ansan, 2009), 66–77.

As a result, donations to Pool now constitute one third of its annual budget. The rest of its budget is raised through project-based public grants, fundraising for shows, education and public program admissions, sales of artworks and publications. The most dramatic achievement of this endeavor was the renovation of Pool's building, which was realized through a collaboration with the artists Choi Jeong-hwa, Sangdon Kim, Sangjin Kim, Kwon Yong-ju, and Suseong Lee. After peeling off the aged substructures of the gallery's interior, we made furniture from the recycled wooden debris and created a garden with seeds collected from neighboring gardens. Acts like this one demonstrate how the Pool community – which is now over 400 people, 120 of whom are registered members – is aware that they are not merely service users but also acting agents of an artist union. In addition to this, I expanded the scope of the Pool community to include curators, gallerists, and amateur collectors. We attempt to get to know one another through sharing meals, having conversations, and taking walks together to artist studios, which I would describe as "critical practices in the life form as art." Indeed, I believe that the quality of the educational and discursive programs proposed by a small art space cannot be exclusively geared towards attracting the general public – it is to this end that a concern with intercontextuality, understood as establishing connections between different kinds of difficulties, lies at the core of our program.

It would be premature to assume that Pool suggests a certain kind of model for the management of small organizations, or for the operating mechanism of any other institution. Pool still functions by gaining grants – even from the national government. Recently, I received a text message from a young artist stating that, "The simple fact that Pool survives and runs actively gives me hope." Younger generations of artists who first experience Pool often describe it as a family, an open discussion lab, or a kind of society where they can find a sense of belonging. On the other hand, older members of the community tend to describe Pool as a space of retreat where they can study, research, and gather. I cautiously call it a "community of lovers," where we can learn ways to respect and care for ourselves, and others.

ASSEMBLIES

Mélanie Bouteloup & Anna Colin

BÉTONSALON – CENTER FOR art and research is based in Paris Diderot University and located in the neighborhood that has undergone the largest development since Haussmann's remodeling of the city.[1] Known as the Paris Left Bank Development Zone, this district's development since 1991 includes the National Library (Bibliothèque François Mitterrand), new streets, transport links, and housing units, as well as the restoration of Paris's flour mill to house Paris Diderot University. Following the transfer of 26,000 students to the new campus – reading subjects that range from social and natural sciences to law, economy, literature, and cinema – Bétonsalon moved into a new space in the university premises in 2007 after four years of activity in two other former spaces in central Paris. The space was allocated to Bétonsalon by the City of Paris, whose ambition was to introduce cultural dynamism within a learning environment.

1. Haussmann's renovation of Paris, or the Haussmann Plan, was a modernization program commissioned by Napoléon III and led by the Seine prefect, Baron Georges-Eugène Haussmann, between 1853 and 1870.

Bétonsalon is the only art center in France to be physically attached to a university but not programmed by it. Taking this context into account, our ambition has been to develop a space of reflection and confrontation at the confluence of art and academic research. By engaging the daily encounter between cultural practitioners, researchers, students, teachers, locals, and the general public, we wish to facilitate the circulation of knowledge and contribute to the university's life and curriculum. Over the years, we have tested out ways of meeting these aspirations through exhibitions, workshops, lectures, seminars, publications, neighborhood tours, festivals, and residencies, all developed according to different time scales and in collaboration with a variety of local, national, and international organizations. If there has been a common aim to these different projects, it is in the wish to set up situations in which diverse interests, disciplines, and singularities learn from, inspire, and unsettle each other in discursive and open-ended formats. By blurring the line between curatorial, educational, and social concerns, we have been committed to giving expression to various discourses, be they aesthetic, cultural, political, social, or economic.

Thus, permeating our activities is the belief that art and its institutions can contribute to the construction and diffusion of alternative discourses, knowledge, and narratives. In the last year or so, the issues raised by the so-called "knowledge society" have been at the center of Bétonsalon's preoccupations. If knowledge has long been recognized as a source of freedom and emancipation, access to it (i.e., to formal education, information, books, and the Internet) not only remains closed to a large proportion of the world population, but is also relentlessly threatened by commodification, as is made manifest in the escalating costs of higher education. Additionally, the fact that the knowledge society gives significantly more importance to material (textual) than to immaterial (oral) knowledge, traditions and know-how further contribute to the erosion of knowledge circulating according to this precept. Under these conditions, the following question has not been settled: will the knowledge society be one of shared or enclosed knowledge?

An example of our approach to and interest in knowledge-sharing across disciplines, histories, and geographies can be found in a recent project, which took as its starting point a radiophonic archive put together over fifty years by an enthusiast named Joëlle Girard, acting under the umbrella name Eldoradio (a collective composed of three radio practitioners including Girard). In July 2010, Bétonsalon was contacted by a member of the GRER (Radio Research and Studies Group) who enquired about the possibility of organizing an exhibition about free radio together with Joëlle Girard and Thierry Lefebvre (radio historian and professor at Paris Diderot University) in the framework of the thirtieth anniversary of the liberation of the radio waves in France. We settled on the idea of inviting a number of researchers and cultural practitioners who would be interested in exploring Eldoradio's archive (composed of some 50,000 recordings, photographs, and press clippings), be it for its quality as an archive that has been formed outside of institutional circuits or for its contribution to the memory of official radio history.

The ensuing exhibition was the fruit of a collaboration between Bétonsalon, the university (professors, students, and alumni of Paris Diderot University), artists, and radio professionals. A group of students in the Scientific Mediation course taught by Thierry Lefebvre, Cécile De Bary, and Richard Millet was also involved in the project from the outset. As part of their assignment, they produced a short documentary about Eldoradio and oversaw the editing of the project's publication, which included scientific and historical perspectives on radio, as well as texts and interviews with the exhibition's participants and with a few key figures of French radio. Each of the invited participants undertook research in Girard's apartment, where the digitized archive is stored. This included L'Encyclopédie de la parole, a group of poets, performers, visual artists, musicians, curators, theater directors, choreographers, and television and radio producers, whose work consists of capturing a diverse range of oral forms. Drawing from a selection of sound recordings from Girard's collection, L'Encyclopédie de la parole created a thirty-minute-long sound piece and wrote a series of captions, which they distributed in the exhibition space. In these, as well as in a live lecture performance, they analyzed eight selected recordings in their own idiosyncratic vocabulary, encompassing different aspects of the spoken word: tonality, pacing, repetition, superposition, compression, saturation, responsibility, and intention. An adept cartographer, poet, and artist, Franck Leibovici undertook the mapping of Eldoradio's archive and of the history of free radio from 1977 to 1981 in France, the period leading up to the liberalization of the radio waves, which was instigated by François Mitterrand's government. This short but crucial moment in radio history was further reflected upon in a visual and sonic timeline that was conceived together with Thierry Lefebvre. The key dates and moments contained in his book *The Battle of Free Radio 1977–1981* (New World Publishing, 2008) were measured against a range of documents (photographs, pamphlets, magazines, law decrees, and radio recordings) once again extracted from Eldoradio's archive. The timeline also covered the adventures of offshore pirate radio stations in the UK that started in the mid-1960s, and the autonomist Bologna-based Radio Alice from the 1970s, thus tracing international connections to France's own history of free radio.

Enabling circulation between history and speculative interpretation thereof, the exhibition and related events further set out to address radio's politics of representation by delving into feminist radio movements and the trajectories of diasporic and trade union-led radio stations in France. While the idea of radio as a vehicle for collective struggles and resistance was one of the exhibition's central concerns, our main focus lay in the different uses and readings of documents surrounding the history of radio, which has yet to be fully written. The diverse contributions demonstrated multiple ways of interpreting and sometimes correcting different types of documents on display – including acts of annotation, retelling, mapping, documenting, and fictionalization – showing that an archive is an object of subjective construction.

Negotiations were necessary at every stage of this project to keep at bay Eldoradio's increasing discomfort towards letting a radio archive be interpreted by non-radio specialists and to be seen as such by the radio world. Most importantly, in the process of collaborating with Eldoradio, it became apparent that the latter had an ambiguous relationship to sharing history: the collective was torn between, on the one hand, making its archive publicly available and allowing it to circulate, and, on the other, a feeling of property and duty of protection towards radio history. As a result, there was an unspoken effort to sabotage any use of this material: access to Eldoradio's archive for the artists and researchers had to be renegotiated every time, while the audio extracts they selected for their respective projects were scrambled so as to prevent their circulation in their original form. In retrospect, the discussions, disagreements, and compromises that arose from this project constituted the most important aspect of our engagement. Indeed, beyond our objective to contribute to the writing of radio history through its reinterpretation within an interdisciplinary approach, we can hope that the conversations held with Eldoradio on the terms and conditions of access and transmission of their archive will impact their future activities and uses of their material.

In fact, key to our modus operandi is the articulation of frictions and negotiations between Bétonsalon and other members of society, and the search for a common ground for different ways of thinking. We are interested in how the process of bringing together heterogenous agents and contradictory opinions can help generate a society of shared knowledge, i.e., emancipated and self-reflexive. Early in the twentieth century, Victor Segalen wrote a plea for diversity against the flattening of the world undertaken by modernity. His *Essay on Exoticism: An Aesthetics of Diversity* (1918) argues that culture is produced through the friction of heterogenous materials. These diverse points of views or singularities can coexist through methods of montage or translation — montage consisting of inserting an object into a chain so that its meaning is modified by the objects placed before and immediately after it. In addition, in her essay "The Language of Things," artist Hito Steyerl links the operation of montage to the one of translation via the use of the term relationalism, thus demonstrating that translation is a tool for emancipation. For her, "translation does not silence the language of things but amplifies its potential of change. [...] It is not about representation at all, but about actualising whatever the things have to say in the present. And to do so is not a matter of realism, but rather of relationalism – it is a matter of presencing and thus transforming the social, historical and also material relations, which determine things."[2]

We saw that one of the prerequisites for the construction and maintenance of an emancipated society lies in the faculty to embrace differences, contradictions, and conflicts. Philosopher Chantal Mouffe coined the expression "agonistic pluralism" to designate this "agonal clash" (to be understood as the multiplication of conflictual spaces where adversaries are not conceived as enemies but opponents), which, far from representing a danger to democracy, is in reality its very condition of existence. We like to consider Bétonsalon as a conflictual space, in which multiple organizations and individuals participate. We see our position as outsiders within the university as constitutive of a way of producing an adjacent yet counter space that can resist the predominant modes of spectacle and standardization. The increasing prioritization of public funds for populist events, coupled with the frequent threats of the City of Paris not to renew Bétonsalon's agreement to remain on its site, keep us in a precarious and fragile position, which prevents us from developing our activities in the long term. In the absence of visionary and receptive cultural policies, the necessity to constantly rethink our modes of action is therefore essential. Beyond our aim to influence national educational and cultural policies, we wish to keep thinking about how to maintain the possibilities of critical assemblies in order to compose an emancipated society of shared knowledge.

---

2. Hito Steyerl, "The Language of Things," *transversal* (June 2006), http://eipcp.net/transversal/0606/steyerl/en.

SELF-INTERVIEW

Beatriz Cavia, Miren Jaio, Isabel de Naverán
& Leire Vergara

BULEGOA ZENBAKI BARIK is a collaborative project involving professionals in different areas. We have taken the platform of this publication as an opportunity to reflect on our project, maintaining the specific character of each of our voices and keeping this visible in our text. To this end, we chose a self-interview format through which each of us formulated and answered several different questions. Editing the interview was limited to putting together the four texts, in the order that they were submitted. What follows is the result of this exercise.

LOCATION
As a small-scale, peripherally located organization, what's your understanding of the idea of working in a specific context?
Bulegoa z/b is located in Solokoetxe, a district in the city center, on top of a hill, which you get to via stairways and lifts. Anyone who makes their way to the area does so for a reason, not just because they're passing by. These features have defined Solokoetxe's character both as isolated and peripheral, whilst also a central and well-connected area

of Bilbao. The topology of the district can be taken as a simile of the topology of the art world, where the binary categories (central/peripheral, isolated/connected, nomad/sedentary, local/foreign) that have conventionally been used to read space turn out to be non-operative.

LOCAL

Bulegoa z/b is a project that came out of a desire to make something that wasn't happening take place in our immediate environment. Our closest accomplice, interlocutor, addressee, support, and context, is the local art scene, which is made up of different groups (performing arts, academic research, visual arts, music, film) that sometimes overlap. Although this crossover has now become natural and essential, in order to understand this situation in relation to the Basque context you have to remember the role that has been played in the past by initiatives such as Arteleku[1] in favoring the dynamics of encounter.

However, the main reason for this crossover of disciplines and interests is due to the smallness of the art scene, and of the Basque Country itself. Our size, which can be a limitation, can also be seen as potentiality: when everyone knows each other it's easier to find one another. Bulegoa z/b has collaborated with a range of local organizations, including publicly-funded institutions and

---

1. Arteleku is an art center located in Donostia-San Sebastián, owned by the regional Government of Gipuzkoa. Since its inception in 1986 and for the most part of the 2000s it was a meeting and reference point for the local art community.

individual initiatives, such as Astigarreta, Azala, Montehermoso, Universidad del País Vasco, La Taller, Solokoetxe Neighbours' Association, and Fuerza Vital.

LOCALISM

No scene is self-sufficient; contact with other contexts is vital. Last autumn we started Bulegoa z/b with the concept of "Forms of Formless Knowledge" and invited initiatives, most of them non-local, that we thought we might be able to use as models for ways of working. At the same time, If I Can't Dance, I Don't Want to Be Part of Your Revolution[2] invited us to work with Isidoro Valcárcel Medina at PiR[3] in Amsterdam.

To take up the simile of topology, you might say that the international art scene is a local one in itself – physical spaces for encounter vary, but the people that meet there don't. The consciousness of localism has grown with the current situation in which the age of networking has given way to the network of support. Our forms of acting and thinking haven't changed, but we seem to have suddenly become conscious that collaboration isn't so much a formal or ethical issue, but actually a matter of survival.

---

2. Based in Amsterdam, If I Can't Dance, I Don't Want To Be Part Of Your Revolution produces artworks and thematic programs.
3. Performance in Residence is a program set up by If I Can't Dance in autumn 2010 that aims to research performances as case studies.

LOCALITY

At the opening of Bulegoa z/b last November 2010 we invited Gora Japon! to play. They played "If I Can Dance," a song they composed for the occasion from the minutes of one of our office meetings. Names of people and organizations mentioned in the document were acknowledged through the chorus of the song. They came from different places (Bilbao, Kurdistan, Vitoria-Gasteiz, Oslo, Madrid, Amsterdam, Chile, London, Seville, Poland), but were intercrossed within the regular structure of a three-minute song.

Bulegoa z/b came out of the different fields of interest, knowledge, and experience of the people who set it up. This has become obvious in its program through relating visual arts, performing arts, sociology, art history, and visual culture. Would you define it as an interdisciplinary venture?
The wish to create dialogue between each of our fields of investigation is what led us to start the project together, thus we've talked a lot about the type of common space we'd like to create out of our relationship and different interests. But we've tried to avoid any kind of labeling right from the start, especially because we wanted to define a space outside of any kind of preconceived model, and to try to focus on our own needs.

In this respect, Bulegoa z/b is a private initiative that came about without anyone calling for it, or encouraging us to set ourselves up as an institution – although at a certain moment it did start receiving public funding. The project began and was defined in answer to a series of differing, concrete needs; among them the need to share our own investigative processes outside of an academic context; to set up new spaces of rupture between theory and practice, to generate new processes of self-education, and possibly to deterritorialize debates, positions, and established forms of generating meaning. We wanted to set up a new space for the production of knowledge that would try to work with its context, but which also generated reflection on its own internal dynamics.

Even though all these needs were very clear from the beginning, we soon realized that each one of us carried with us certain concrete forms of institutionalization from previous experience (from the academic context, from public art institutions, etc.) This often surfaced in seemingly minor ways. For instance, when we were putting out the chairs and tables for each event, we realized that the way we were placing them was creating a bigger distance between guest and audience. Now we try out new ways of organizing the space each time. This can be taken as an example of how Bulegoa z/b is a structure that defines itself through its own urgencies.

If Bulegoa z/b takes these concrete needs as a starting point, what kind of public responsibility do you consider you have?

Bulegoa z/b's public responsibility is also directly related to its private sphere; that is, to the personal needs, desires, and frustrations that have motivated our lines of investigation and content from the beginning. One of our "unmentionable" desires is to set up an independent study program – a model that doesn't exist in the Basque Country. It might not be a possibility at the moment, particularly because of financial limitations, but the dynamics we've set up in our first year of existence have been working in that direction. In this respect, Bulegoa z/b currently works to support processes of self-education that are open to the public.

Would you like to become a producer of art projects?
No.

Do you find the idea of production interesting?
We find the institutional or organizational production of art projects interesting because we think it is a practice that requires urgent revision. We were talking about this recently with María Mur, the director of Consonni, a Bilbao producer. Our conversation came about after a public presentation of the glossary that we commissioned Isidoro Valcárcel Medina to make. The glossary is a kind of beginning for a practice we'd like to develop, which consists in choosing a series of terms or concepts and inviting people from different areas to put together activities based on them, allowing us to observe different ways of relating to the same concepts. The meanings of concepts are often taken for granted, and with this practice we want to question their usage and meaning. This is how we became interested in discussing, amongst many others, the concept of production. So we thought of inviting María Mur, as Consonni (an independent

organization based in Bilbao since 1997) defines itself as a producer of art projects.

Although you haven't organized that debate yet, you say that production is a concept that requires urgent revision. What have you observed about it, and why does it interest you right now?
Our aspiration with Bulegoa z/b is to produce discussion, reflection, and the exchange of ideas. We've sometimes spoken and discussed the "production of knowledge" – what it means in current terms, and especially, by whom, or where it happens/takes place. This is directly linked to our concern with education and the transmission of knowledge, but this is an area of discussion in its own right.

We have observed that production – whether artistic or theoretical – is often understood merely as funding. Institutions appear as coproducers of projects, but hardly know anything about their content. In most cases there isn't a close relationship (be it supportive or conflicting) between the different partners involved in the development of a project, and yet satisfactory results are expected. This leads to the current situation where, even in art practice, production is relegated to a neoliberal function of production and consumption. In spite of this, there are also a lot of initiatives where this doesn't apply. Initiatives that are interested in production, but that also become spaces for discussion; where projects can be contrasted as they're being carried out, thus effectively working as coproducers. They don't necessarily finance projects, but they do nourish organizational processes. In Bulegoa z/b we're interested in these other models because we find them more enriching and stimulating.

Bulegoa z/b proposes a kind of redefinition of the relationship between theory and praxis. How do you understand your activity of reflecting on this relationship, and how do you approach it in your daily work?
Under the shelter of the academic world, arising from different life histories and working backgrounds, as well as different networks and local contexts, Bulegoa z/b has been built up over its lifetime by different emergencies. We might speak of two directions or angles in the way we conceive the relationship between theory and praxis: on the one hand, from the positions that we articulate and, on the other, from the position we situate our project in. The first direction would lead us to think of this relationship as a theme in itself, as an idea and form of discursive elaboration of the world of art and contemporary thinking. From the second angle we would accentuate the process of the construction of this relationship, considering it as an action in itself.

From one angle we draw different perspectives: working with/from theory – manipulating, learning, managing, disseminating, and modifying it. Theory as the material of our work, reflection, dialectics, and construction. Theory as the nucleus, where we converge.

The second angle identifies that this relationship is constantly being carried out through Bulegoa z/b. We contruct our identity through different activities, thinking, ideas, impulses, relationships, and links. We propose, we accept; we discuss, we act. The project takes shape. It's performed. It's even archived.

In our case, the relationship between theory and praxis is articulated through our daily work, which is itself founded on a consolidated theoretical background. From the idea we had when we started out – when we trusted that sharing a common space would turn something pragmatic into something productive – to the present moment, where we've established certain dynamics in our work and reflection that are acted out, Bulegoa z/b has built itself up as a working model by four women whose aims and lines of investigation are forged during the process itself, and not exclusively by an aim we set ourselves, or others set for us.

There's one aspect – the fact that we come from parallel disciplines that overlap – that introduces a kind of strangeness and tension to the two ways in which we understand the relationship between theory and praxis. That is, with regard to reflecting on their relationship, because each discipline favors different aspects of theory. Declassification, post-colonialism, feminism... whichever theoretical approach one uses to circumscribe these concepts, they're highlighted in different ways by the visual arts, sociology, the performing arts, or cultural critique, and these forms of emphasizing assume certain methods, implications, situations, or approaches. Discussing the assumptions and implications of these ways of focusing in a particular art context like that of the Basque Country defines Bulegoa z/b's specific lines of work. There's also a tension in the actual carrying-out of this endeavor: because praxis in the art world differs from scientific praxis, because action in art and science follow different formats and methodologies, because formats answer to canons, conventions, tendencies, and/or concrete paradigms. And, finally, because whatever all this brings to light creates dichotomies that we continually need to work out – investigation *vs.* creation, art *vs.* science, theory *vs.* praxis – which we must use to think about and model ourselves on.

LOSING CONTROL

Francis McKee*

WHEN I GOT THE JOB at CCA the whole place was dead on its feet – it was empty and it was bankrupt.

This was a very pompous building, a huge building for a tiny organization. It had cost ten million pounds to revamp it, the largest lottery-funded building in Scotland, and it was dead. So we tried to turn offices into art spaces and to put the emphasis back on art; to take it away from bureaucracy and retail and the business plan which comes with these things. I was quite obsessed with open-source programming at the time, and thought, "Let's make this an open-source program and an open-source building."

We couldn't afford to program all the spaces, but thought that if we gave some over to other people and offered it to them on a different basis, they could use it. So we began to do that – making collaborations and partnerships – and people

* This text is based on excerpts from the Circular Facts: Public Meeting in which Francis McKee was speaking on a panel with Nataša Petrešin-Bachelez and Norma Jeane, moderated by Mai Abu ElDahab, on the subject of "How to Work," focusing on how artistic practices inform institutional methodologies.

would come with all sorts of ideas and we would give them space to do things. And if we could support them in different ways, we would help them with marketing and technical support – we would say, “As long as you don’t need money, because we don’t have it!”

And then there’s a core program – which is what we do – although we’re even beginning to think of giving that away. Our whole policy looked very weak to funders: they said, “Where’s the curatorial control? This is a hippy gesture, how can it work economically?” But it did work because there was more momentum and there were more people using the space and because we weren’t saying, “We’re commissioning you to do this and that.” People were organizing projects for themselves. So they began to feel ownership of the space.

At the same time, we started a gardening program. We had been working in Red Road Flats in the north of Glasgow with about sixty different populations living there, and sixty different languages. We rented buses for them to come to CCA for the final exhibition, but no one would get on the bus! But they all came to the bus and they all talked and then they all went home again. It was a real lesson. At moments like this you think, “Those people are never going to come to the city center and come to us.” We responded by going to them and getting out of the CCA building. We thought of gardening because most people in Glasgow don’t eat many vegetables, so the average mortality rate in some areas is about fifty. You can’t actually get fresh food in a lot of areas. The project began with giving people the opportunity to grow vegetables and to learn more about gardening. We then made a connection to seeds, the way they are copyrighted, and the whole notion of intellectual copyright, and then open source. Again, that program took place in public spaces and we wouldn't come in a patriarchal way and say, "We will grow you a vegetable." Later we turned one of the rooms at the CCA into a greenhouse and started growing plants ourselves. These were simply put on tables so people could take them away; we subsequently started making exhibitions about gardening as well.

We're trying to give away control. With this in mind, the next step is to have a steering committee of all the people we work with regularly so we're no longer in charge of everything. There's obviously still some kind of curatorial management in opposing dictatorial curatorial control but the real challenge is in stepping back, to make other things happen. (Andy Warhol's factory seems to have worked precisely because Warhol did not intervene – a courageous approach to management.)

Also in terms of our situation, the Arts Council no longer exists, there's a new entity called Creative Scotland, which insists it isn't a grant-giving body, nor a cash machine. They're there to make strategic investments across the country in terms of festivals and intellectual exports from Scotland. So we have to figure out what we want to do, why we want to do it, and then how we make them agree to let us do it. That seems like a better way to function in this new environment than to succumb to the rhetoric of creative industries. There's always a pressure to become a really thriving "business." We don't necessarily want to be one; we don't want that kind of ethos if it obstructs or obscures the core desire to create new artwork or support artists.

The organization itself though can easily become quite punitive in its operational mode. An arts organization is an organism that would prefer no audience. That's the ideal every organization works towards if left unchecked: its natural status, its ecstatic point, when it's empty and therefore running completely smoothly. The challenge there is to work against that entropic movement, to destabilize that action.

On the question of funders and their desire for public interaction, when it comes to the general public I don't know what/who that is. Is it two middle-aged people with two kids? I don't know who the general public are, but I know that we address a coalition of niche audiences. We do Gaelic music and poetry, and probably only people who speak Gaelic will come to that. If we do Sisonke, which is an African festival, the audience is probably going to be African asylum seekers. If we do an exhibition, then God knows, it will depend on the kind of exhibition. Recently we displayed a cast of a drowned body and lots of people just to came to see "the dead body." Very Glasgow-ish! So it's really hard to predict; it's impossible. We do many different things and have many different publics coming.

We try to be professional – for example, we're talking about things like how to be better at customer care. But at the same time, there's a certain amount of chaos and if we get too far beyond that chaos it will probably be bad for the ethos of the space again. When it gets really professional, that's when it can become punitive. I think people tolerate a certain amount of us not being rigidly organized. Once, for instance, we were screening a movie and waited for someone to park his car because his wife was already in the cinema. We waited the extra twenty minutes until he had parked! It's not going to kill anybody, it's not totally professional, but who cares? The audience, by the way, was very supportive of the gesture and no one complained.

It's not unknown for artists to say that things are not good enough; for example, you build a screen and a room and they turn out a little wonky, so you have to go and rebuild them. It's something that can happen, but we try to get things right as much as we can. Indeed, there is a high standard of visual presentation demanded and provided by CCA. The audience however is perhaps more likely to say we're unprofessional based on occasions where we've sometimes opened an exhibition late so that the artist can get it finished. Admittedly, there is a sort of looseness present, but it's a looseness springing from a desire to get things just right rather than being sloppy.

We don't always succeed. I don't think anyone ever does, from what I hear. Failure is acceptable to audiences at times if it reflects a high degree of ambition or a desire to create a more open ecology in a space.

We are trying to support artists as well. We've tried different programs to support and provide development opportunities for artists and curators. We help artists do practical things, such as creating a budget for the first time. So we're trying to introduce more professional practices in terms of administration for artists, structured learning for interns, and residency space for the development of new work.

We were lucky when we had our financial meltdown in 2005. We were forced to confront central questions when others were complacently receiving their funding. No one asked them, "Why do you exist?" We were asked because our funders really didn't believe that we should exist. That was quite healthy because we had to think carefully about what the point of our existence was; what we could usefully provide for artists and audiences. Having to answer these questions compels you to consider your role and relevance. If you can answer them convincingly, then it's easier to explain to others why you should exist. Then you can change their opinion rather than have to adapt to their ideology.

Beyond Representation

Conversation between Kim Einarsson and Emily Pethick

EMILY PETHICK: Circular Facts began not long after The Showroom reopened in a new building in the Church Street neighborhood of London. Throughout the project we have simultaneously been adjusting ourselves to a radically different local context, as well as reassessing our relationship to the London art context – thinking about what is necessary in terms of how to support artists and how to enable discussions and production that is not taking place elsewhere. As a result, our program has shifted towards foregrounding collaborative and process-driven approaches to production, partly in response to our new local context, as a reflection of my own interests in this kind of production, as well as the fact that no other London organization is consistently focusing on this area. Having previously worked at Casco – Office for Art, Design and Theory in Utrecht, I have retained an interest in how one can simultaneously work very locally and produce work that remains interesting and useful to a wider international context.

You recently took over as the director of Konsthall C, another small arts organization, that is situated in a suburb of Stockholm. Can you tell me a bit about the background of Konsthall C? How was it set up and what is its specific local context?

KIM EINARSSON: Konsthall C was initiated as a public artwork in 2004 by the artist Per Hasselberg in collaboration with the Municipal Council of Hökarängen. The Municipal Council is not a public authority, as you may think, but an umbrella organization self-initiated by the residents of Hökarängen. It serves as a forum for various local associations and organizations in the municipality, like schools, sports clubs, and tenants associations.

The suburb of Hökarängen was built in the late 1940s, and was organized according to the neighborhood planning ideals at the time. By placing the houses in smaller neighborhoods with their own center there was a hope for increasing social interaction between the inhabitants. Hökarängen consists of five neighborhoods, and Konsthall C is situated in one of those, in a so-called "center building" of such an area. The "C" in Konsthall C stands for Center, and the building still contains communal services like a laundry room, a youth center, a school, and artist studios. According to the utopian concepts of Swedish community planning of the 1940s, the Municipal Councils were conceived as local political and social forums on a grass-roots level, but the concept was never fully realized. In the General Plan of 1952, the proposal to introduce the Municipal Council concept was removed, primarily out of fear that the capital city would break up into decentralized and unruly little enclaves. However, in 2003 a number of Hökarängen residents reassembled the idea of the Municipal Council as a way to gain influence over their suburb, and the establishment of Konsthall C became an important part of this process.

Per Hasselberg, whose artistic research was specifically focused on the democratic processes of postwar politics in Sweden, met with the initiators of the Municipality Council and the public housing companies of the area. Together they decided to set up an art space in a former shared laundry room offered by the public housing company and called it a Konsthall. Both the concepts of the Konsthall (and cultural institutions in general) and the shared laundry room (a shared space where you come and do your laundry, rather than having private washing machines in your apartment) play significant roles in the discourse of the Swedish model – they were seen as important instruments to foster a democratic and communal society.

All the meetings and negotiations were an important part of the development of Konsthall C as an artwork as well as for Hasselberg's artistic practice. As a result, the Municipality Council became the owner of the artwork Konsthall C. After running it for a couple of years curator Niklas Östholm took over as director and Anna Livion took up the post just before me.

EP: While Konsthall C essentially started off as an artwork, it has since evolved into an art center that has a broader function. Can you talk about how the program has developed and about the current focus of Konsthall C?

KE: Since 2003, Konsthall C has had several directors but I think one can identify a common focus on research-based processes and a broader attention towards social planning, politics, and economy. In the beginning, the programming was very closely related to the artistic research of Per Hasselberg, which focused specifically on Swedish aspects of democracy and the almost utopian ideas of the neighborhood planning of the late 1940s and 1950s. To generalize a bit, my predecessor Anna Livion and I have both tried to maintain the link to the specific history of Hökarängen, Konsthall C, and the building itself, but also connect this history to global and contemporary discourses and tendencies, for instance in projects investigating processes of privatization and the selling off of the welfare state. Even though Konsthall C has developed into an institution or art center, I still think of it as an ongoing research project, where the projects are more or less obviously linked to each other.

One of the many questions I am interested in investigating is how to work *with* politics as an art space and cultural organization, i.e., how can we go beyond just representing political struggles or just making political gestures.

EP: My experience of working in small organizations – and the reason why I keep working in them – connects very much to what you describe: the possibility of creating a situation that allows for development, for an organization to evolve, change and learn through the work it does, i.e., often through the work we are producing – engagements with artists, audiences, and others – we learn something as an organization, or make new relationships that lead to other things. I have tried to avoid creating institutional structures that restrict the work, and instead try to allow the work to have an influence in shaping the institution, rather than the other way around. I am also interested in how an organization may act politically beyond representation – rather than just speaking or describing, how can it act in a micro-political sense. I've found that quite often the way that this works is in the finer details of a project, so I am wondering if you have any specific examples where this has happened.

KE: I think this happens on very different levels and in different kinds of activities. I don't want to label certain actions as political, since that presupposes some sort of a definition or a fixed understanding of what a political act is – which is impossible, since it is so tightly connected to specific moments and situations. Having said that, I think it is really important that we try to share practical experiences, and try to find a new vocabulary to address the ways in which we, as cultural organizers, make the sustained effort to problematize and change the order of things.

On an organizational level, I think that this happens in how we consciously distribute our engagement, money, and time. For example, by making sure that artists always get paid and by providing them with good and interesting working conditions. We also have a feminist policy; in practice, this means that we want to keep a gender balance in favor of women not only when inviting or employing artists, graphic designers, carpenters, curators, lecturers, etc., but also with regard to how money is distributed.

I think that a lot of the political work is done in the way that we organize our work – for example, by discussing how the division of labor can be adjusted to our different life situations. We try to engage actively with discussions on our present cultural policies and future funding systems, by giving direct feedback to the funding bodies and politicians. Sometimes it can be complicated to bite the hand that feeds you, but I think that these are important roles for any publicly-funded art organization, especially in a time when neoliberal cultural policies attempt to direct us toward entrepreneurial management and private funding.

In our actual program, I think that a lot of what we do sets out to problematize our understanding of the radical and the political, not only as general topics, but also in relation to what goes on around us. One question that permeates a lot of what we do is when and where political work is actually carried out. When it comes to specific works I think that they operate on several levels that go beyond the descriptive or representative: sometimes as calls for action, as in the case of the handbook and the utopia workshops developed by Malmö Free University for Women (MFK); sometimes as a catalyst for discussions, like Petra Bauer and Annette Krauss's project *Read the Masks. Tradition is Not Given* (2009). The format of the political is not predetermined – it may reside in the way the work unfolds or is narrated but also in the places where it operates.

By using different temporalities, levels of participation, having time-consuming processes, allowing failures, collaborating with a number of different groups, and experimenting with formats, we look for the strongest possibility to do something beyond representation.

As I see it, running a discursive program and maintaining a place that simultaneously enables and empowers new communities, while strengthening already existing ones, is an important part of our political work. Artists, activists, political organizations and associations, collectives, and magazines often use the exhibition space as a place for their meetings – sometimes as part of our program and sometimes not. I like the idea that the physical space of Konsthall C (once a communal laundry room) can continue to be used as a communal space, even though the washing machines are gone.

In April 2011, as part of the aforementioned project by MFK, the artist Annika Eriksson was invited to work with their handbook. In turn, she invited one of her students, Celie Ekholm, who, also in turn, invited the Palestinian activist Leila Khaled, who became world famous in 1969 for hijacking airplanes.[1] Nowadays, Khaled works mainly with women's rights in Jordan. Bringing her to Sweden caused a lot of media attention from right-wing politicians and journalists, who claimed that we had invited a terrorist using taxpayers' money. The issue was brought up in parliament, and the cultural minister had to comment on it. Unfortunately, the public debate around the event got limited to this, and we as an institution failed to initiate a nuanced political debate. However, the incident made it clear that all the different groups and individuals organizing and participating in the event had very different motives and expectations surrounding the invitation of Leila Khaled.

By collaborating with MFK, I wanted to investigate how Konsthall C could be used as a place for feminist and political activity; Annika Eriksson wanted to invite a female political icon; Celie Ekholm, who also is an activist, wanted to invite someone she admires as a friend and person; some of the audience wanted to meet a legend, some wanted to hear a politician; Iaspis wanted to support a Swedish artist (Annika Eriksson) to fulfill her project, etc. Inviting Leila Khaled was definitely not a political action, but it triggered a highly political situation. Furthermore,

---

1. Leila Khaled is a member of the Popular Front for the Liberation of Palestine (PFLP). She is currently a member of the Palestinian National Council. On August 29, 1969, Khaled was part of a team that hijacked a flight on its way from Rome to Athens, diverting the Boeing 707 to Damascus. In 1970, Khaled was involved in the attempt to hijack a flight from Amsterdam to New York City. The attack was foiled, the plane diverted to Heathrow, London, and Khaled was caught by the police. Later the same year the British government released her as part of a prisoner exchange.

the negotiations and reactions around it made clear how the popular conception of the art space as "non-political" or neutral can be used to reallocate resources. The local Swedish Palestine Liberation Organization, PLO, office later pointed out how hard it would have been for them or any other political organization to invite a person like Leila Khaled to Europe, and how this only could be made possible in the name of art.

EP: Something that we both have in common – and with many other spaces of our scale – is the approach of community building through our programs, both in the sense of serving the local artistic community, and the neighborhood. Can you describe the relationship(s) you have with the public(s) around you a bit further?

KE: For me, community building is one of the reasons for running an art space today. I'm not interested in running a pleasure ground for passers-by on Sunday afternoons. There's nothing wrong with that, but I prefer having continuous dialogues and creating relationships with a number of different groups. Our audience consists of a number of very different communities, which sometimes overlap. Bringing together different groups with common interests creates an interesting space to work within. We recently held two seminars in relation to texts on critical theory by Wendy Brown[2] – artists, academics, activists, and journalists were invited to discuss the texts in small groups and later with Wendy Brown herself.

In the feedback that we received it was pointed out how rare it is that people from these disciplines come together and discuss the relationship between political theory and practice.

I'd say it is impossible to really talk about a local audience. Our collaborations with organizations from our neighborhood have quite different audiences. We run a film club together with one of the local tenants associations, which mainly attracts elderly people living in the area; at the same time, we also collaborate with the Allotment Association (we have a small garden patch for artists and others to work with) and the People's Kitchen (a local group of young activists who cook), whose frequenters are younger and from all around the city.

EP: I think the possibility for these different kinds of activities (which range from discussion about political theory and practice to people's kitchens) to coexist in a fluid way is one of the things that distinguishes spaces such as yours and that makes them really exciting. There is a desire to find some kind of mutuality or common ground with the users of the space, to build communities around it and create a more informal, concentrated and intimate situation of exchange. In this sense, having a small audience and being relatively hard to get to,

---

2. Wendy Brown is a professor of political science at the University of California, Berkeley. She has made major contributions to post-Foucaultian political theory, critical legal studies and feminist theory. Her research addresses problematics of political power, political identity, citizenship, and political subjectivity.

can actually be a benefit. However, given the current pressures on the public sector all over Europe, it seems that spaces that operate on this scale may well be under threat in the future. Sustainable in the long-term or not, what are your thoughts for the future of Konsthall C, in a realistic or idealistic sense?

KE: In a realistic sense, I am not very hopeful. The pressures on the public sector are really noticeable in our daily work in all kinds of ways. This may be a sidetrack, but it is interesting to note how despite the fact that the annual budget of Konsthall C has been almost the same since its foundation, the number of funding bodies that sustains it has increased considerably over the years. What worries me the most at the moment is the tendency of increasing bureaucratic control and demands for private funding from both politicians and funding bodies, and the general reluctance to support risky projects. I think it will be hard to run our current program in a couple of years, if things don't change radically.

Ideally, I wish Konsthall C to remain as a small-scale organization, so that it can directly reflect the interests of the people engaging in it, unlike larger organizations having to standardize their practices. As you pointed out, the strength of our institutions is the ability to simultaneously work very locally while running projects that could be useful to a wider international context. Certain aspects of these institutional frameworks – such as people getting paid, professional support for those involved, being part of an international network – do create the possibility to make projects that are defined by critical, political, and visionary engagement while encouraging and sustaining a personal and immediate connection with their contributors, partners, and audiences.

BUREAUCRACY IN OSLO

Will Bradley

I'M GOING TO APPROACH THIS in a somewhat unorthodox way, but still, I hope, connected to what Emily initially suggested.* The question of institutional authorship: how, who, what, or where you are affects what you are able to say, and the related questions of power and of responsibility. So first of all, is there somebody here who speaks good French and could read something for me?

A member of the audience reads the following lines:

> *Ta voix, tes yeux, tes mains, tes lèvres, nos silences, nos paroles, la lumière qui s'en va, la lumière qui revient. Un seul sourire pour nous deux, par besoin de savoir.* [Suddenly realizing what they are reading] ... It's poetry! *J'ai vu la nuit créer le jour sans que nos changions d'apparence. Au bien-aimé de tous, et bien-aimé d'un seul. Au silence de ta bouche, a promi d'être heureuse. De loin en loin est la haine, de proche en proche est l'amour ... de notre enfance.*

---

* This text is based upon excerpts from the Circular Facts: Public Meeting in which Will Bradley was speaking on a panel with Dan Kidner and Giovanni Carmine, moderated by Emily Pethick, on the subject of "What We Do." The session looked at possibilities of defining the authorial position of institutions, and the implications of this position of authority. The following text is an excerpt from the panel.

Yes, it's poetry, a surprise attack by poetry. And what I'd like to ask is, did anybody die after that? [*Most people in the room seem entirely unmoved.*] And if not, then how do you feel? What effect did it have? I ask because in another context, these lines are represented as having incredible power. They come originally from Paul Éluard's *The Capital of Pain* (1926), but in this adapted form are spoken by Anna Karina in Godard's well-known film *Alphaville* (1965). This is the poem with which Anna Karina's character Natacha von Braun destroys the all-powerful computer Alpha 60 in a revolutionary paroxysm, and overturns the totalitarian society of Alphaville.

What I'm interested in here, from the point of view of institutional authorship, is the difference between what happened, or failed to happen, when you heard these lines just now, and the utopian possibility that they unleash as a plausible, powerful part of the fiction of *Alphaville*. We can invest in this beautiful moment as performed by Karina and framed by Godard, and we are led to a position that allows us to believe, or to wish to believe, that those words could *in themselves* change the world as dramatically as they promise to. That art might have that extraordinary power. Yet, as we demonstrated here just now, in another context, framed differently, they can pass by almost without trace.

The American musician Iggy Pop offered a slightly different approach to the same question. He was unhappy with David Bowie's original 1973 mix of the Stooges album *Raw Power*, and he remixed it for its re-release in 1997. So when he was asked what the problem with Bowie's version was, he said:

> *This is the problem with the original mix of* Raw Power. *By the time I finished* Raw Power, *my standards had become different from other people. That's the only way I can put it. I wanted the music to actually come out of the speakers, grab you by the throat, knock your head against the wall, and just basically kill you.*

This is what the first mix of *Raw Power* was unable to achieve, to Iggy's ears. What's salient is that he doesn't consider the possibility that the music does not, in some psychotic altered universe perhaps, have at least the potential to knock your head against the wall and just basically kill you. Back in 1973, he was convinced that the potential existed, and that it was defeated by Bowie's institutional authorship.

So I wanted to begin with these extreme examples of investment in the impossible; in some extreme transformative power that something we might call art can, in certain circumstances, be imagined to possess.

And against that I wanted to set some version of what we do, in our small-to-medium-sized, more-or-less independent, contemporary art-focused quasi-institutions. In other words, I want to talk about bureaucracy, which is a large part of what we do. So the second half of this short presentation will be about how and why we engage bureaucracy.

At another seminar not entirely unlike this one, the filmmaker and activist Florian Schneider answered the question about why we do what we do very well. My memory is (I can't cite him exactly), that he said more or less that it's obvious that we are anti-capitalists and we are hedonists, and in that case what should we produce? We should produce pleasure for ourselves, and problems for capital. This was then augmented by the idea that of course we believe in the avant-garde and so we want to imagine *new* pleasures and *new* problems for capital. And the extraordinary difficulty that this uncovers is that everything we do in these kinds of organizations is almost totally unsuited to producing either of those things. So now the question on my mind as somebody who, for the first time in my life, has a job with one of these small-to-medium-sized organizations, is whether there is any imaginable possible accommodation between this idea, this ambition, and the practicalities: the bureaucracies, the flights, hotel rooms and train times, the funding structures, the audience figures, the white paint on the walls, the advertisements in international journals, the evaluative workshops – which all, at some point, seem to get between us and the objective.

We opened [Kunsthall Oslo] in September 2010, and already it seems to me that we're in an impossible position. In order to succeed as an institution, to survive bureaucratically, we have to fail to throw ourselves wholeheartedly into the maelstrom of utopian impossibility, and this is really a desperate situation to be in. What would, of course, be more interesting would be to fail to become an institution at all. And paradoxically that *is* a practice – to produce a position of institutional authorship that would be a constant problematization of the conditions of your institutional existence; a continual failure to become what, bureaucratically, you must become. But, of course, as everybody here knows, as soon as you go down that path, your imagined power is removed because you are part of a wider system; you are only living by its grace. So my unreachable ideal is that the question of institutional authorship is the question of the impossible construction and futile defense of a space that is antagonistic to capitalist bureaucracy, even though it is only on the terms of capitalist bureaucracy that it exists. I want to feel that I'm stealing something from it, and it wants to feel that it controls me. One of us must lose.

Kunsthall Oslo is not exactly an institution. Nobody asked for it, nobody wanted it; it's illegitimate. It has no constituency, no de facto institutional standing, and very little expertise. It's largely an artifact of public-private property development, constructed in a new financial zone on the site of Oslo's former industrial harbor. In order to explain to the world that what Norway does now is no longer fishing and knitting, but global capital management on a vast scale, a deliberately iconic financial zone is being built in the form of a series of skyscrapers. From the side, these narrow buildings, finished predominantly in either black or white, depict a giant barcode, and the development is called the "Barcode." Or it was until the developers started to sell apartments in some of the towers, and then the area was renamed as the "Opera Quarter," because it's easier to sell penthouses in the "Opera Quarter" than in the "Barcode."

The majority of primary property developers involved are all actually owned by the state. However, the ultimate owners, and any long-term profits from the development, are predominantly privatized. This "third-way" approach, the skewed public-private partnership familiar from two decades of post-Thatcherite development in the UK, is relatively new in Norway, but is now the governing paradigm for urban development.

And Kunsthall Oslo's place in all this is as a public artwork. One of the conditions the city set for the construction of this new financial zone was that it should make provision for public space, or in Norwegian *allmening*, which has "common land" as its closest English translation. And this was interpreted as the idea that the ground floor of all of the new buildings should be open to the public in some form. What the developers were most obviously thinking of is the typical gentrified landscape of cafés, restaurants, and fashion shops. But currently it's a half-built new financial zone on what was formerly the site of container storage, a railway siding, and the warehouse district. Right now there's nothing there at all of public interest.

Though Kunsthall Oslo is right next to platform nineteen of the central station, nobody would walk down our street if they weren't working on the construction of the Norwegian headquarters of Visma and Den Norske Bank. So right now we are the only expression of this idea of *allmening* in the area.

How did this come about? The city mandated culture in this not-yet-built zone, and approximately two million euros was allocated to produce public sculpture. At this point, there was a moment of agency where the developers were persuaded that a new independent art institution would be a valuable public artwork in the context. This move was unpredicted in the initial plans, and led to the creation of Kunsthall Oslo as an anomaly in the overall picture; a piece of the *allmening*, a sliver of common land that extends from the pavement into the commercial landscape, with an uncertain future. We are, of course, still completely instrumentalized by our creators, who value the ideas of "liveliness" and "place-making" for the future success of the overall development. Originally, to recognize this fact and also to point towards a more utilitarian idea of art production, we planned to call the space "Instrument," which works very well in Norwegian. But the board controlling the initial funding wanted to instrumentalize the space much further than that. "Kunsthall Oslo" is a name that is much more useful to the developers than "Instrument," and so we lost this public reference to our situation. Now we're left both with this situation, and this fake idea that we are a kunsthall. But I should also emphasize, in case this short description gives a misleadingly bleak idea of our situation, that we have substantial public funding from both the City of Oslo and the Norwegian Arts Council, and operate according to a constitution that mandates both our artistic independence and non-profit status. Still, we have to dig ourselves out of our particular initial position somehow. Or else, more likely, we have to fail to do so in the best way we can.

I'm trying to inspire a change of heart. My invocation of Éluard could maybe be misunderstood as a cynical gesture, but what I hoped to show was that, though Éluard's words have no power here, Godard is able to make it appear as if they have incredible power, and so in some sense (and not least in Raymond Williams' materialist sense of amplification) amplify them and give them at least the latent power of utopian belief. So I suppose what I'm actually trying to say, or propose, is the opposite of cynicism. Going back to Emily's initial question about institutional authorship, I'm trying to say that this is the work that is required of us. From the stupid and compromised positions we're in, the impossibility of even stating the utopian case is the problem we're up against, and facing its imaginary failure, is the impossible job that I still hope we're trying to work on. We are striving – in any way that's available to us as "institutional authors" – to close the gap between the kind of flat situation that Éluard's words produced on this occasion, the failure of that work here, and between the kind of extraordinary power that Godard is able to give to Natacha von Braun's reading of the poem in *Alphaville*, where in that moment it seems clear and obvious that twenty lines of Paul Éluard can bring down the state. And that's not cynical, is it?

THE A AND B OF KUNSTVEREIN

Krist Gruijthuijsen & Maxine Kopsa

A: WE STARTED KUNSTVEREIN not so much as a reaction to the global financial crisis, but more as a reaction to the current cultural climate in Amsterdam. For about two years prior to our opening in 2009, we'd been feeling an increased need to see and show artwork and art practices that were otherwise simply unavailable in the city. At the time both the Stedelijk Museum and de Appel were closed. Of course there were galleries up and running including those profiling young talent, and the important artist collective W139, but there was little on offer in terms of spaces more focused on mid- to late-career, internationally conscious retrospectives, as well as longer running, weightier solo shows. Put differently, Kunstverein arose out of a personal need for a smaller venue, one more low-key in terms of operating structure and also more open to criticality. Furthermore, one that would be ambitious enough to be able to fill an institutional gap that would show museum-like projects on an intimate scale.

B: So this aim was both personally driven as well as fed by a local lack.

A: We were excited about new venues, most of which were coming out of New York City. These were venues that doubled as studios or ateliers, showing progressive work on a concentrated, low-key scale with a careful, investigative attitude (for example Dexter Sinister, Orchard, Dispatch). This is not to say that Amsterdam (or the Netherlands) was, or is, hopelessly lagging in terms of discourse and cultural stimulation, specifically in terms of visual art. Instead, Kunstverein began out of a positive need and sense of necessity to fill gaps and initiate or excite a discourse.

B: But that was then.

A: Indeed. Those were happier times. The situation has since changed quite drastically. Where ten years ago we were worried about Amsterdam being a city where production and support was (pragmatically) rampant, and only five years ago we were witness to a city where the visual arts were slowly becoming increasingly neglected – again, with the Stedelijk Museum and de Appel closed – we were simply missing institutional clout on various levels. Just recently – since June 27, 2011, to be exact – there has been a complete transformation.
An unreserved, unabashed, unmitigated burial.

B: Our right-wing government has officially decreed the small institution, site of production and experimentation, dead; the production house, experiment, dead. By cutting the funding going to presentation venues in half, and removing the support to postdoctoral research such as that developed in De Ateliers, the Rijksakademie, and the Jan van Eyck, this cabinet has ripped out the heart of cultural activity. Without the middle ground – the arena traditionally most supportive of (younger) experimentation – the Netherlands will slowly experience a cultural meltdown. Larger institutions – the ones actually far more capable of generating private funding – have been spared. For now, so have the academies. But who will present all the artists, dancers, and musicians previously supported by smaller institutions?

A: In recent years, the absence of an institution such as the Stedelijk Museum has certainly contributed to the popular support received by the VVD Secretary of Culture for his shameful cuts: an entire generation has grown up without its didactic foundation.

B: If the so-called midriff of the arts disappears, that is, places that sustain and instigate presentation, advanced academic research, and grants for artists, there will not be nearly as much space for investigation, experimentation, and cultivation. To think this will stimulate a competitive (read: healthy) environment is ridiculous and short sighted.

A: I'm happy that the chair of the National Cultural Advisory Commission (the committee responsible for advising the government on its cultural policy) has quit. Someone has to say that we can go only so far.

B: But let's get back to Kunstverein and to the question of viable models for small art spaces. KV started off in a nineteenth-century apartment, a domestic environment, where we imagined a visitor might feel right at home but would still enjoy the tension set up by the parameters of a public exhibition/event. Ascending several flights of stairs, our visitors entered into an intimate salon setting that defined Kunstverein as a meeting place and as the site of a new community. The venue itself was rich in terms of the history of Dutch artistic communities – the original owners of Ruyschstraat 4 were well-known for their efforts during the Second World War in sheltering artists threatened by the Nazi occupation. Years later, the fourth floor apartment also housed the studio of the city's official sculptor. Our first exhibition was a "retrospective" of Ian Wilson that included a discussion as well as rare physical works: the discussion took place in the otherwise empty space; a day later, we installed his *Circle on the Floor* from 1968 and one of three paintings from 1966 that he had reconstructed from memory in 2006. In many ways this show established the discursive line that would follow through the rest of the program. This and "The Hypnotic Show" that followed it, curated by Raimundas Malašauskas – a one night only session in which descriptions of the works "on view" were read out by a hypnotist, and could only be experienced when under hypnosis – were important for us to set up Kunstverein's "stage," so to speak.

A: In 2010, after we had been open for a year and a half, we felt that it was time to move on and to challenge the idea of an ideal audience once again. By employing the model of a *kunstverein*, and its use of a membership structure, we deliberately played with notions of inclusivity and exclusivity from the start. We began by introducing an existing structure, namely the *kunstverein* model with a membership system as its basis, in order to research what an ideal audience could become for us. Who would become a member and why? What does the membership imply for us? By working with this model we knew we would be able to create a community from scratch, made up of people directly committing themselves, so to speak, to the program. We were interested in targeting and working through word of mouth, instead of trying to get the masses in. Of course the masses were and are welcome – in fact anyone can visit Kunstverein, whether a member or not. But, generally, we felt that the time called for an alternative to programming for mass audiences; that instead we should offer concentrated presentations to feed local, national, and international audiences. Our members are mainly artists, curators, gallerists, collectors, and institutional directors. Our current audience includes such professionals as well as passers-by, especially since our move to the store-front location.

The storefront location we currently inhabit is more approachable and more easily accessible. However, it was imperative that Kunstverein maintained some of its domesticity and persisted to advocate and adjust the notion of presentation. The store rethinks a model of representation through the usage and function of a *shop-economy*. Again, allowing the context of its location to feedback into its program, Kunstverein hosts a series of survey shows of radical, yet underrepresented artists, that look like everyday shops. Right now we have a retrospective of the work of American writer, visual poet, artist, critic, and editor Richard Kostelanetz, which is a bookstore for all intents and purposes. Everything in it is for sale. For reasons closely connected to Kostelanetz's practice, we felt it was consistent that Kunstverein become a bookstore dedicated to the artist, as a more viable alternative to a straightforward retrospective. Kunstverein then became "The Robert Wilhite Design Store," showcasing the practice of an artist who has made flatware, furniture, props for plays, paintings, and sculpture. "The Robert Wilhite Design Store" also functions as a proper store. The idea is that this setting not only affords an intriguing backdrop for the practice on view, but also attracts different audiences without losing the original one.

B: It's a way of blending in while still keeping a certain amount of autonomy.

A: During the last year, Kunstverein has concentrated on investigating the idea of and depicting art history's blind spots. Overlooked and/or underrepresented historical figures that have provided a great contribution to the knowledge of art production form the core of our program. Each of the protagonists has a strong (personal) need to express their, often radical, position: one that demonstrates a true commitment and dedication towards artistic production – whether socially, economically, and/or politically related. Either too specific in their niche (Ben Kinmont's quiet practice, for example), too multidisciplinary (Kostelanetz and Wilhite have both been notoriously difficult to pigeonhole), or too avant-garde (precisely these practices that are witness to categorization difficulties), most of these artists have been widely ignored by larger Dutch and international art institutions.

B: We are constantly reshaping and rethinking the necessity of our existence and feel that this is the responsibility of every (smaller) institution. Not that all places of presentation should only be encouraged to work through a constant experimentation with their structure; nonetheless, they should be questioning its viability. KV tries to uphold the notion of *urgency* not only for ourselves, but in terms of art (historical) display. We thus aim to provide the utmost visibility for initiated projects by collaborating with various international institutions. All in all, Kunsteverein's conceptual focus concentrates on the relation between domesticity, self-organization, social commitment, and even *bravery* in art production.

A: We have had the luxury of being able to give ourselves the freedom of such experimentation with the possible flipside that the whole could stop at any time. Kunstverein's program is supported financially by the contributions of its gold members, and through grants from public and private institutions. Due to the fact that our respective incomes do not need to be generated from Kunstverein, we were from the outset at liberty to create a space that didn't rely on a money-generating configuration. This liberty is also one we firmly aim to extend into the general makeup of Kunstverein: there's no need to follow the usual five-week show rotation and no reason to spend more than a healthy amount on PR costs (all information is sent digitally through an expansive e-mail directory and, other than the occasional e-flux mailing, we advertise in the local gallery agenda). We force ourselves to stop whenever we sense that we're getting stuck in a rut.

B: It's interesting that freedom is often something more difficult to hold onto than, say, convention. You'd think it would be simple to stay clear of "curatorially-correct" attitudes or of a certain accepted language. But these are pitfalls into which one can somehow naturally fall.

A: It was important to create a model that seemed truly natural to us and to test it by doing; altering it when we felt it needed tweaking. I mean "natural" in terms of scale and self-organization (we wanted to be able to oversee everything ourselves), programming (it is crucial that we maintain this feeling of necessity in the program – of answering to a lack), and flexibility (we need to be able to adapt to changing social and political dynamics). From the beginning, Kunstverein was conceived as a franchise model outside its time-honored German-speaking context that aims to reshape and remodel the traditional institutional format of the *kunstverein*, without any tangible connection to its cited "big brother." In addition to Amsterdam, there are now two other branches: New York and Milan.

B: Here again, it was a collective desire to work transnationally that gave birth to the idea of the *franchise*. As a franchise, Kunstverein establishes an ongoing dialogue amongst its various branches but the curators of the respective Kunstverein's are responsible for their own program. However, what does unite us directly is Kunstverein Publishing. Under our broader framework of necessity and urgency, publications are produced when a need is encountered either art historically or by more local demand. The books (including the in-house magazine called *Ginger&Piss*) are not seen as explanations of the program but a distinct, equally significant body of work. The publication is an exhibition venue in itself that is able to transmit the ideas of art presentation spatially and temporally.

A: Moreover, by way of a distinct and specialized voice in publishing – where our publications carry a strong voice in terms of design and reflect the particulars as opposed to the general in the program (small runs, detailed topics), Kunstverein is able to contribute to an international discourse (as everything is published in English and distributed worldwide) from a small-scale but agile position.

B: This agility is the key. Every smaller institution has it, in varying degrees, but it's easily forgotten – before you know it, the structure that you created has turned into a monster and is in control of you. As Richard Kostelanetz said, "I never collaborate with more than one other person; three can get out of hand."

A: He might have a point. Keeping things small or close to home keeps them responsive and more likely to uphold any original engagement.

B: We aim to remain nimble. Kunstverein will continue to respond to a *climate*, be it cultural, economic, and/or political. Those parameters will define its future.

SITUATED

Nataša Petrešin-Bachelez*

LES LABORATOIRES D'AUBERVILLIERS is situated in Seine-Saint-Denis, one of the poorest banlieues of Paris. This area is notorious for its social instability, which includes high levels of unemployment, a disenfranchised youth, one of the highest rates of illiteracy in France, and was one of the sites of the 2005 youth riots. After the Second World War the area was declared part of a red zone, being one of the suburbs that had historically been run by the Communist Party. Today Aubervilliers is home to more than 100 different ethnicities, and a large percentage of its population does not speak French, which brings a very interesting energy to the area.

This context establishes Les Laboratoires as one of the prominent examples of art institutions located outside of the center of Paris. An increasingly lively artistic landscape has developed in the outskirts of Paris over the last decades, with

---

* This text is based on excerpts from the Circular Facts: Public Meeting in which Nataša Petrešin-Bachelez was speaking on a panel with Francis McKee and Norma Jeane, moderated by Mai Abu ElDahab, on the subject of "How to Work," focusing on how artistic practices inform institutional methodologies.

the addition of several contemporary art centers, theaters, etc. However, for people who live in Paris, Aubervilliers is on the edge of the world, which results in Les Laboratoires not having a regular public, and few passers-by, which is something that we try to address in the way that we work, as I will go on to describe.

Les Laboratoires is based in a former light metallurgy factory, whose activity was abandoned along with some other factories as part of the partial deindustrialisation of the area from the 1970s onwards. During the 1980s the mayor of Aubervilliers was the Communist politician, Jack Ralite, who was a great amateur of art and theater in particular. He decided to give the factory over to artists, and invited the choreographer François Verret to shape the artistic direction of the space in 1994. Verret used it as a rehearsal space for his dance company, but also invited other colleagues – mostly performers and choreographers – to use it as well. In 2001, a collective directorship was established following Verret's and other artists' collective engagements in the space, and art historian Yvane Chapuis, curator and critic François Piron, and choreographer Loïc Touzé, were appointed as co-directors.

For this reason, there are several determining factors with which we work at Les Laboratoires, the most important being that the directorship is always collectively run; at least one of the directors has to be an artist; and that it is a residency place for artistic research projects. In 2010, a new team of directors was formed, which was comprised of Alice Chauchat, who works in conceptual choreography and is interested in processes of sharing that are inspired by the free software movement; Grégory Castéra, a curator who specializes in contemporary dance and performance; and myself, a curator with a visual arts background and a heightened interest in the notion of artistic research and knowledge production through artistic practices.

When we arrived a year and a half ago our aim was to continue to focus on residencies that are concentrated on artistic research. Les Laboratoires has always been understood as a flexible tool that is adaptable to the proposals and needs of the artists we invite. This means that it's versatile in terms of its budget, time, and even in expectations. For example, the artist does not necessarily have to produce a final product – the emphasis of the work is on the research processes themselves.

As artistic directors we are also particularly interested in the free software movement as a model for artistic production, particularly in relation to how spectators might become active participants in a research process. For example, as soon as a public event takes place there is an audience expectation that it is a performance, a product that is closed and final; by creating space for discussion before and after the events, we build in the possibility of sharing ideas with the audiences and of receiving more immediate feedback from them. But although we often work with different kinds of participatory practices, we remain conscious of the danger of how these can be instrumentalized by organizations to give the appearance of fulfilling their social responsibilities. For this reason, an important component of the research residencies is the way in which they address local publics. This happens in various ways through exchanges that take place between the artist and a variety of local actors, workers, or inhabitants. We try to find ways in which these moments of exchange and sharing can be properly mediated, in formats such as workshops, lunches, dinners, association meetings, but also more formal discursive events.

Finally, we often find interlocutors for specific research projects. For example, the Slovenian artist and architect Marjetica Potrč worked at Les Laboratoires for two months, and was looking for a collaborator for her research on biodiversity and multiculturalism in Aubervilliers, linking the two with the wish to create what she calls "an ephemeral monument to Aubervilliers." We introduced her to an Aubervilliers-based PhD student who was studying landscape architecture as well as involved in a local theater group, and has also done a PhD in biodiversity. At Les Laboratoires our desire is to enable these kinds of magical moments when human resources, relationships, and the sharing of knowledge – without hierarchies – can happen and endure.

One of our funders has criticized us for having no "red line" in what we do, and for having "atomized" audiences. However, we think that these qualities are part of the strength of what we are trying to achieve when addressing the "situatedness" and the "locality" of Les Laboratoires. The variety of projects and public events, which result from the theoretical or artistic research that we engage with, will never attract or address the same kinds of publics. And why should they?

SMALLNESS

Mai Abu ElDahab, Binna Choi,
& Emily Pethick

TO TALK ABOUT SMALL institutions is to talk about a way of working rather than a question of scale, be it physical or institutional. Working intimately with artists, choosing the parameters of our relationship to the politics of representation, and being flexible yet professional, is what differentiates us from museums or artist-run spaces. In his text "Take Care," Anthony Huberman profoundly says that perhaps smallness is in *how we behave* as institutions. Circular Facts, as a collaborative project involving five small organizations, enabled us to behave in the deliberate and reflective way in which we believe artistic production, artists, and our audiences should be supported.

With the legacy of Institutional Critique in the background and "New Institutionalism" in the foreground,[1] many of the texts in this publication and surrounding Circular Facts, express a deep hesitation in using the term "institution." Tarnished by its implication in power politics, the institution today often takes on the look and form of intelligence and academia, but in reality sticks to tried and tested formats and vocabularies of exhibitions and discursive activities.[2] In contrast, Circular Facts tried to operate within a framework of mutual support, resourcefulness, and responsiveness in order to realize diverse projects that

---

1. A term coined by Alex Farquharsen that identified institutional practices that espouse to operate with a self-reflexive criticality. See "Bureaux de change," *frieze* 101 (September 2006).
2. Sven Lütticken suggests "New Institutionalism" can be seen as "a solution that has quickly become part of the problem." Rather than self-critique, it often functions as a tool for self-legitimation. See "Once More on Publicness: A Postscript to *Secret Publicity*," *Fillip* 12 (Fall 2010).

required very different methodologies, skills, and knowledge. We like to think of our smallness as coming from this shape-shifting, which is embedded in a desire to learn, enabling us to coproduce thoughtful and meaningful projects. Equally important are the rewarding personal relationships fostered throughout the project, which were a carefully considered and key element to its success.

It seems to be quite natural, therefore, that the project's name, Circular Facts, was derived from one of the artists, Ruth Buchanan. *Lying Freely* (2009–2010), a project by Buchanan and the first produced by Circular Facts, was developed in an itinerant form, each stage taking place in a different location and involving three different forms of address: a guided tour, theater piece, and two exhibitions. Informing the way in which we wanted to work together as organizations, her project's evolution through encounters with local organizations and contexts embodied our attitude towards our collaboration. *Lying Freely* was also an attempt to find a way of negotiating privateness and publicness, a balance which we are in search of as well. Hence, instead of establishing a touring package of exhibitions, Circular Facts evolved through its encounters with different institutional environments and their local contexts.

Through our discussions, we realized that each of our organizations was concerned with the notion of institutional authorship, and that this questioning may well be a distinctive feature of our "smallness," reflected in the practices of artists we are working with and the tone of our institutional voices. Norma Jeane is an artist who uses a pseudonym as the author for her collaborative projects involving fields outside of the arts. This characteristic of Norma Jeane's practice streamlined with our desire to engage with non-artistic knowledge and generate spaces where different expertise can breed new alliances and experience. Norma Jeane's research within Circular Facts was into modes of participation in public space and was developed through several actions produced with different artists, their target partners and audiences, and under the umbrella of an ongoing project entitled *For Real!* (2010–). Norma Jeane's ideas and position regarding authorship, as well as her deliberate and practical realization of research, helped us consider the meaning of our positions as authors, as well as reflect on what a research-based practice can be or effectuate.

A reticence towards claiming authorship and ownership is also reflected in the practice of the Brussels-based organization Agency's ongoing research into hesitations in relation to questions of intellectual property inline with open source ideology. Beyond our three organizations, it is clear (particularly through the essays in this book) that this interest in open source logic extends to Les Laboratoires D'Aubervilliers, Bétonsalon, CCA Glasgow, and Konsthall C, who have each expressed desire to broaden institutional space into a communal one.[3] In essence, Agency's prac-

3. Francis McKee, director of the Center for Contemporary Art in Glasgow, participated in the Circular Facts: Public Meeting where he introduced us to the model they are enacting where the users (staff, artists, and the public) determine the nature and activities of the institution.

tice within Circular Facts is an educative tool that informs our organizations and helps us consider our position towards intellectual property and copyright and its relationship to our work and roles within the cultural field. Notwithstanding, Agency's practice is a crucial investigation into the impact of market-driven regulation of art, which stands very much against our understanding of independent practice.

This open source approach extended to the way in which some of the artists that contributed to Circular Facts chose to work with us, using our structures as sites of production as well as research. Artists Ei Arakawa, Gela Patashuri, and Sergei Tcherepnin used our invitation to develop plans for a new center for contemporary art in Tbilisi, Georgia, constructing musical instruments through which models for the space were performed and amplified. The three iterations (at Casco, The Showroom, and CCA Bretigny) have been envisioned as "instruments" on many levels: to contribute to (or interfere with) Circular Facts, as an instrument for the Tbilisi artistic community, as well as quite literally being musical instruments. Beyond this, the artists stressed the importance of visiting the organizations and learning from them in order to research and develop their own organizational model, in so doing productively instrumentalizing the opportunity.

Turkish artist Can Altay's projects within Circular Facts took on issues of instrumentalization head on. Beyond the policies for "social cohesion" in the respective cities of London and

Utrecht, Altay looked for different forms of partnership and cohabitation. Making use of each organization as para-institutional venues, the emphasis of his research was in conflicts and negotiation. His *Church Street Partners' Gazette* (2010) involved the participation of many different people who live and work in The Showroom's neighborhood and looked at notions of boundaries and communities, partnership and transformation, building many new local links and partnerships for The Showroom. Through *COHAB: an assembly of spare parts* (2011) at Casco, Altay extended this research into cohabitation to think about the 400 or so public sculptures that are placed in the city of Utrecht. Altay was interested in the tension between how these have been placed by the local authorities versus how they are lived with, and then sought for a way to renegotiate these relationships. This involved collaborations with different local stakeholders, including the municipal authorities and in particular those workers who physically placed the sculptures.

While Altay's project demonstrated an embedded approach to working within a specific locality that activated different kinds of collaborations, Petra Bauer's new film *Sisters!* (2011) evinced an even more exhaustive approach within this vein. The film was made in collaboration with another small organization, the London-based radical feminist group Southall Black Sisters, who actively campaign for the improved position of women and for the preservation of secular spaces within the public sector. Key to Bauer's approach is linking those who share some affinity over similar issues, but in a way that does not push for a consensus or singular modus operandi. Through its cross-sectoral approach, the film and research around it created an opportuntity for the organizations in Circular Facts to look into the urgent questions around women's positions within the ongoing European debate on multiculturalism. Furthermore, it enabled us to think about how artists and art organizations can engage with this, importing this knowledge into our own circuit of action.

Realizing two consecutive solo exhibitions in very different spatial and institutional conditions, Hassan Khan took the opportunity to experiment with exhibition formats and institutions' working methods, and take a new turn in his practice, producing new sculptural (rather than audio-visual) works, through which he addressed narrative structures. His exhibitions both stemmed from investigations into formal cues that regulate the relationship of the viewers to works on display, and presented several types of narrative structures unearthing the subtleties of cultural nuance. In juxtaposition with the other projects within Circular Facts, Khan's practice allowed us to think about how to challenge exhibition models, and delve into the relationships between form and narrative.

In the current political-economic climate one cannot deny that vulnerability is a consistent attribute of our smallness. The challenges that we currently face are not only connected to the shrinking of the public sectors in our home countries, but broad repercussions of this on independent work. Curator Dan Kidner pointed out during Circular Facts: Public Meeting that "the pockets of resistance or pockets of possibility for independent and critical thinking are getting smaller and smaller." Under these conditions, we see Circular Facts not just as a vehicle to coproduce new work, but as an invaluable opportunity to bring a group of "small" visual arts organizations into closer contact and dialogue and to make these relationships public, open to scrutiny and transformation. The public meeting and the texts in this book have helped us identify some key common agendas amongst organizations and curators today, finding where our affinities lie, and recognizing the common difficulties we face. The vital "smallness" of our organizations is a working ethos and position that enables the development of critical and complex artistic endeavors that can be nourished, expanded, and widely circulated. This could well be the circular fact that we are purporting.

CONTRIBUTORS

Mai Abu ElDahab is director of Objectif Exhibitions, Antwerp.

Mélanie Bouteloup is co-director of Bétonsalon – centre for art and research, Paris.

Will Bradley is curator of Kunsthall Oslo.

Beatriz Cavia is a social researcher and lecturer at the University of the Basque Country EHU/UPV, and is a member of Bulegoa z/b, Bilbao.

Binna Choi is director of Casco – Office for Art, Design and Theory, Utrecht.

Anna Colin is co-director of Bétonsalon – centre for art and research, Paris.

Kim Einarsson is director of Konsthall C, Stockholm.

Krist Gruijthuijsen is co-director of Kunstverein, Amsterdam.

Anthony Huberman is a curator and writer based in New York, a visiting professor at Hunter College, and director of The Artist's Institute.

Miren Jaio is an art critic and lecturer at the University of the Basque Country EHU/UPV and a member of Bulegoa z/b, Bilbao.

Heejin Kim is director of Art Space Pool, Seoul.

Maxine Kopsa is co-director of Kunstverein, Amsterdam.

Francis McKee is director of CCA, Glasgow.

Isabel de Naverán is a researcher in performing arts, a member of ARTEA, and a member of Bulegoa z/b, Bilbao.

Emily Pethick is director of The Showroom, London.

Nataša Petrešin-Bachelez is a freelance curator and critic based in Paris and, with Gregory Castera and Alice Chauchat, is a co-director of Les Laboratoires D'Aubervilliers, Paris.

Leire Vergara is a researcher and independent curator and a member of Bulegoa z/b, Bilbao.

Published by Sternberg Press

Editors: Mai Abu ElDahab, Binna Choi, and Emily Pethick
Publication Coordinator: Marnie Slater
Copyeditors: Mafalda Dâmaso, Emily Pethick, Natasha Tebbs, Kate Stancliffe
Proofreader: Leah Whitman-Salkin
Transcriptions: Debbie Herring
Design: Kaisa Lassinaro
Printing: Die Keure, Belgium

ISBN 978-1-934105-65-8

Casco – Office for Art, Design and Theory
Nieuwekade 213-215
Utrecht 3511 RW
The Netherlands
www.cascoprojects.org

Objectif Exhibitions
Kleine Markt 7-9/bus 26
Antwerp 2000
Belgium
www.objectif-exhibitions.org

The Showroom
63 Penfold Street
London NW8 8PQ
United Kingdom
www.theshowroom.org

Sternberg Press
Caroline Schneider
Karl-Marx-Allee 78
10243 Berlin
Germany
www.sternberg-press.com

This publication is published on the occasion of Circular Facts. Circular Facts is a collaborative endeavor between three European contemporary art organizations: Casco – Office for Art, Design and Theory (Utrecht); Objectif Exhibitions (Antwerp); and The Showroom (London), in partnership with Kunst Halle Sankt Gallen and Electric Palm Tree.

Circular Facts has been made possible with the support of a Cooperation Measures Grant as part of the European Union Culture 2007–2013 Programme. This publication is additionally supported by BAM, the Flemish Institute for Visual, Audiovisual and Media Art; Arts Council England; the Mondriaan Foundation; and Utrecht City Council.
www.circularfacts.eu

Culture Programme Education and Culture DG
Mondriaan Stichting
Gemeente Utrecht